AF228165

EXPLORING NATURE

Spotting Trees

BY ANGELA LIM

Kids Core
An Imprint of Abdo Publishing
abdobooks.com

abdobooks.com

Published by Abdo Publishing, a division of ABDO, PO Box 398166, Minneapolis, Minnesota 55439. Copyright © 2026 by Abdo Consulting Group, Inc. International copyrights reserved in all countries. No part of this book may be reproduced in any form without written permission from the publisher. Kids Core™ is a trademark and logo of Abdo Publishing.

Printed in the United States of America, North Mankato, Minnesota.
102025
012026

Cover Image: Shutterstock Images
Interior Photos: Yulia Raneva/Shutterstock Images, 4–5; Leena Robinson/Shutterstock Images, 7; Shutterstock Images, 8, 25 (top left), 25 (top right), 25 (middle right), 25 (bottom left), 28 (bottom right), 29; Xi Xin Xing/Shutterstock Images, 9; Nancy Kennedy/Shutterstock Images, 11; Monkey Business Images/Shutterstock Images, 12; Uwe Bergwitz/Shutterstock Images, 14–15; Roman Khomlyak/Shutterstock Images, 17; Rozova Svetlana/Shutterstock Images, 18; Ovidiu Hrubaru/Shutterstock Images, 20–21; Teresa Otto/Shutterstock Images, 23; Anna Kucherova/Shutterstock Images, 25 (bottom right); Nikhil Patil/iStockphoto, 26; Le Do/Shutterstock Images, 28 (left); Stephen B. Goodwin/Shutterstock Images, 28 (top right)

Editor: Marie Pearson
Series Designer: Marley Richmond

Library of Congress Control Number: 2025939171

Publisher's Cataloging-in-Publication Data

Names: Lim, Angela, author.
Title: Spotting trees / by Angela Lim
Description: Minneapolis, Minnesota: Abdo Publishing, 2026 | Series: Exploring nature | Includes online resources and index.
Identifiers: ISBN 9781098298746 (lib. bdg.) | ISBN 9798384932543 (ebook)
Subjects: LCSH: Trees--Juvenile literature. | Forests and forestry--Juvenile literature. | Dendrology--Juvenile literature. | Nature--Juvenile literature. | Ecological science--Juvenile literature. | Habitats (Ecology)--Juvenile literature.
Classification: DDC 583.6--dc23

CONTENTS

Many people enjoy playing in autumn leaves.

CHAPTER 1

Changing of the Seasons

Nathan chased his older brother Drew down a trail in the park near their home. It was a crisp fall day, and the leaves were just beginning to change colors. Nathan stopped to look at a tree with bright-yellow leaves.

When Nathan looked back at the trail, he almost couldn't find his brother. Drew was hiding behind a huge tree trunk! Nathan ran to catch him.

"What took you so long, slowpoke?" Drew teased.

Nathan pointed behind him. "I got distracted by that yellow tree."

"I've been learning how to tell the difference between types of trees in school," Drew said. "Do you want to take a look with me?"

Nathan nodded. The two of them went back up the trail. Drew bent down and picked up a leaf from the ground. To Nathan, it looked like a bunch of leaves.

Some trees turn yellow in the fall. Others turn red, orange, or other colors.

A compound leaf has many smaller leaflets.

Drew explained that it was a compound leaf. Small leaves called leaflets were connected to the same central stem. Drew pointed out the toothed pattern that ran down the edges of each leaflet.

"It's an ash tree," Drew decided from these **observations**. He felt confident because he knew these trees tended to change color early in the fall. Drew was proud to put what he had learned to use. But Nathan seemed less impressed. He raced away, kicking up yellow leaves as he went.

Leaves fall off of certain trees during autumn. They can be raked into a pile to play in.

What Is a Tree?

Trees are a type of plant. All trees have woody **tissue** that makes up their trunks. Trees come in many sizes. Some can be hundreds of feet tall! Others may reach only 2 inches (5 cm) tall. Different trees have different leaves. Leaves can differ in shape and edge **texture**. The leaves of some trees change color and fall off every fall. Some trees have leaves that stay green year-round.

Palm Trees

Many people think of palms as a type of tree. But these tall plants are more like grass or bamboo. The hard covering on the trunk of a palm is not bark. It is dried tissue from leaflike structures called fronds.

Some trees, such as crab apples, grow beautiful flowers in the spring.

Learning to identify trees can take time. But people do not need to travel far to learn about these plants. Trees grow everywhere from forests to big cities. With practice, people can learn to name the trees around them.

Lauren Marshall works for the Arbor Day Foundation, which plants trees. Marshall talked about the importance of trees:

> Research suggests that being around nature in general and trees specifically, is really helpful to your mental health.

Source: Erica Van Buren. "Trees Are Proven to Lower the Temperature in the Environment and in People's Moods." *Augusta Chronicle*, 28 May 2024, augustachronicle.com. Accessed 21 Feb. 2025.

What's the Big Idea?

Read this quote carefully. What is its main idea? Explain how the main idea is supported by details.

Trees can grow in cool,
northern places such
as Alaska.

CHAPTER 2

Where Trees Grow

Different trees grow in different **habitats**. They grow in certain **climates**. Temperature and rainfall affect the types of trees that can grow in a region.

Many trees need a lot of water to survive. Forests grow in places with a lot of rain or snow.

The Hoh Rain Forest in the Pacific Northwest receives about 12 feet (3.7 m) of rain each year. Douglas fir and western hemlock trees are common in this forest.

Other US forests receive less rain. They may get 2.5 to 5 feet (0.8–1.5 m) of rain annually. These are temperate deciduous forests. Trees such as oaks and maples are common there.

Elevation

Temperatures are cooler at high elevations. The air is also drier. This can make it difficult for trees to grow. Tall mountains have a tree line. The tree line is the elevation at which forests can no longer grow. The few trees growing above the tree line are spread far apart. They may not grow to their full height.

Because of all the rain, trees in the Hoh Rain Forest are often covered in mosses.

Grasslands and deserts get little rain. However, some trees can survive with little water. Cottonwoods and willows grow near bodies of water in grasslands. Junipers grow in the desert.

Tree roots hold down soil and prevent it from washing away.

Soil

The type of soil affects the kind of trees that can grow. Trees and other plants tend to grow best in loamy soil. Loamy soil is rich in **nutrients** and holds water well. Fruit trees, spruces, aspens, and more grow in loamy soil.

Sandy soil has a rough texture and does not hold water well. But many trees can grow in this type of soil. Oak and poplar trees are two examples.

Clay soil is tightly packed and becomes sticky when wet. It is difficult for air and moisture to seep through clay soil. Birches, elms, and sycamores grow well in clay soil.

Further Evidence

Look at the website below. Does it give any new evidence to support Chapter Two?

Temperate Forest Habitat

abdocorelibrary.com/spotting-trees

People can see coast
redwoods at Redwood
National and State Parks
in California.

CHAPTER 3

Identifying Trees

Trees may look similar. But there are clues people can look for to help with identification. One clue is size. Coast redwoods are some of the tallest trees in the United States. They can grow to be more than 320 feet (98 m) tall.

The crown of a tree includes its leaves and branches. Some trees have wide crowns. The crown of a bur oak has a width of about 60 feet (18 m).

Leaves

Deciduous trees lose their leaves during the fall. They usually have broad, flat leaves. Evergreen trees keep their leaves year-round.

Looking at Bark

Bark color and texture can help people identify trees. Sycamore trees have splotchy, multicolored bark. Birch trees have white bark. The bark peels in horizontal strips. Shagbark hickories have vertical strips of bark that look like they are peeling off the tree.

Some evergreens have thin, pointy leaves called needles. Other evergreen trees have scales. These leaves are made up of small, overlapping structures. Still others have broad leaves.

Different leaves grow on different types of trees. Broad leaves come in many shapes. Some are compound. Compound leaves have many leaflets that connect to a central stem.

Walnut trees have compound leaves. Other trees have simple leaves. A simple leaf is made of a single leaf blade. Most maple trees have simple leaves.

Leaf edges can help people tell trees apart. Magnolia leaves have smooth edges. Leaves from elm trees have toothed edges. Some oak leaves have lobes. These are rounded parts that stick out.

Flowers and Fruit

Some trees flower in the spring. Redbud trees have small clusters of pink flowers. Magnolia trees have large, cuplike flowers. The petals vary in color. They can be pink, white, yellow, and more.

Leaf Shapes

The shape and edge of a leaf can help people identify trees.

Fruit is another thing to notice. Oak trees have acorns. Maple trees grow winged seeds that are commonly called helicopters.

Sketching or tracing the outline of a leaf can make its shape easy to look up later.

Spruce trees have cones. Apples, pawpaws, and buckeyes are other examples of tree fruits.

Trees may look similar at a quick glance. But it is possible to tell them apart. People can take a notebook outside. They can write down

what they notice about a tree. They can sketch
a leaf. Later, they can use field guides, online
resources, or mobile apps to identify the tree.
Trees are important parts of nature, and they
are all around!

Explore Online

Visit the website below. Does it give
any new information about trees that
wasn't in Chapter Three?

Unbeleafable

abdocorelibrary.com/spotting-trees

Field Notes

Tree Identification Log

Name of tree:
Pin oak

Location spotted:
Pin Oak Prairie, Minnesota

Date spotted:
June 28

Type of leaf:
Broad leaf

Leaf shape:
Lobed

Leaf color:
Green

Sketch of leaf:

Bark color and texture:
Grayish brown with shallow grooves

Flowers and fruit:
Acorns

A blank Tree Identification Log is available at abdocorelibrary.com.

Glossary

climates
areas with specific weather patterns

elevation
the height above sea level

habitats
the natural environments where plants or animals live

nutrients
substances that living things need to grow and stay healthy

observations
information gathered from the senses

texture
the way a surface looks or feels

tissue
a group of cells that work together to serve a specific function

Online Resources

To learn more about trees and tree identification, visit our free resource websites below.

Visit **abdocorelibrary.com** or scan this QR code for free Common Core resources for teachers and students, including vetted activities, multimedia, and booklinks, for deeper subject comprehension.

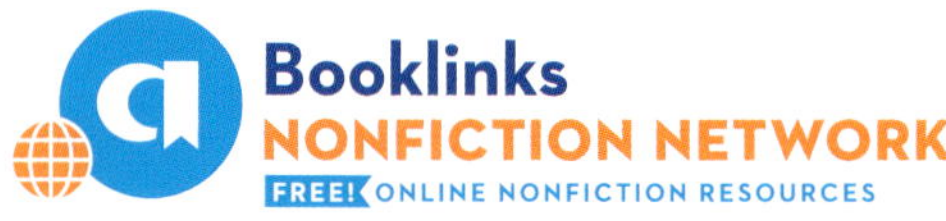

Visit **abdobooklinks.com** or scan this QR code for free additional online weblinks for further learning. These links are routinely monitored and updated to provide the most current information available.

Learn More

Brower, Felicia. *A Kid's Guide to Backyard Trees.* Gibbs Smith, 2025.

Hoare, Ben. *The Secret World of Plants.* DK, 2022.

MacCarald, Clara. *Forest Biomes.* Abdo, 2024.

Index

About the Author

Angela Lim is an MFA student in poetry at
Indiana University.